THE

indistractable

WORKBOOK

Welcome

If you've ever sat down to tackle something important, only to find yourself scrolling, swiping, or snacking— you're not alone.

In a world designed to be endlessly engaging, staying centered on what matters can feel like a constant uphill climb. Between the interruptive notifications and ever-growing to-do lists, it's easy to feel overwhelmed and reactive.

Distraction happens to all of us, and it's not a personal failing or character flaw. With the right strategies, you can regain control of your attention and align with what matters most.

What You'll Find Inside

In this workbook, you'll discover tools to help you gain clarity on your distractions, uncover the root causes behind them, and design a system that protects your time.

Step-by-step exercises

We'll walk through simple, actionable practices to help you reset your routines, follow through on what matters, and build the identity of someone who does what they say they will.

Science-backed strategies

The tools in this workbook are grounded in decades of behavioral science, from psychology to neuroscience to cognitive research. They're built on the same evidence-based methods I share in my bestselling book, *Indistractable: How to Control Your Attention and Choose Your Life.*

Instead of generic productivity tips, you'll gain a framework that is research-backed and proven to transform how you manage distraction.

A customized approach

We'll guide you through tailoring these tools to fit your life and goals, giving you space to reflect and build your own version of success.

How to Use This Workbook

The pages in this workbook are designed to be action-oriented. You can work through the sections in order, or skip ahead to the parts that feel most relevant.

There's no one "right" way to work through this, but here are a few principles that may help:

1. Before you dive in

Find a quiet spot to read and reflect. Give yourself permission to be fully present by turning off your phone and shutting the door.

2. Be honest, not perfect

You don't need to impress anyone here. These prompts are for you. The more honest you are about how you spend your time—and what gets in your way—the more value you'll gain from this process.

3. Check in with yourself

Progress won't always feel dramatic. Remember that small changes compound and lead to transformative results over time.

Congratulations! You've already taken the first step to becoming indistractable. I'm so glad you're here.

Nir

What's Your Superpower?

At a glance:

★ **Intentional living means eliminating distraction.**
Achieving the life you want involves not only doing the right things, but also resisting actions that lead to regret.

★ **The problem is deeper than devices.**
While devices often get blamed, distraction arises from more fundamental psychological drivers.

★ **Traction starts with the root cause.**
Before you can move forward, you need to understand what's pulling you off track.

★ **Four steps form the Indistractable Model.**
Mastering internal triggers, hacking back external triggers, making time for traction, and preventing distraction with pacts form the core framework of becoming indistractable.

★ **Being indistractable is the superpower of the century.**
In a world full of diversions, the ability to stay in control of your attention becomes a rare and powerful skill.

What's Your Superpower?

Distraction often pulls us away from what truly matters. Scrolling before bed, checking your phone during work time, or spending a whole evening on a TV show may not seem like a big deal. But when these habits repeat every day, they create a significant impact. Bit by bit, they take us away from our goals, our relationships, and even our values.

It's easy to blame devices, but turning them off doesn't fix the problem for long. When I deleted social media apps from my phone, I just spent more time reading headline news. When I canceled my streaming subscriptions, I started visiting the pantry more often. The form of distraction changes, but the result is the same: lost time and regret.

Feelings like boredom, stress, tiredness, or worry often trigger the urge to escape. Quick distractions bring fast relief but don't last, which is why digital detoxes or avoidance strategies rarely work. To break the cycle, we have to notice the root causes that drive distraction.

Mastering attention, therefore, becomes one of the most important skills in modern life, and your capacity to guide it directly shapes what you accomplish. You finish your work instead of putting it off. You give your full attention to people you care about. You take care of your health by keeping promises to yourself.

This skill isn't something you're born with—it develops through practice. By observing your distractions honestly and learning to handle the discomfort underneath them, you build strength over time. The world will always send new diversions your way: Tomorrow will bring more alerts, more content, and more demands for your focus.

The advantage goes to those who resist the pull of distraction in favor of choices that match their values. To be indistractable is to exercise that power—the ability to decide how attention is spent, no matter what competes for it.

Exercise 1

You're at the very beginning of this journey to gain back your focus and attention.

What would becoming indistractable mean to you? What will you be able to do that you've never been able to before?

Let's Chat! With Nir

Why do I keep getting distracted even when I want to focus?

Distraction is part of being human. We tell ourselves we'll do one thing, but then something else pulls us away. Sometimes it's our phone or email, but often it's something as simple as boredom or stress.

The reason it happens is that distraction feels like relief in the moment. That relief might only last a few seconds, but the brain remembers it and seeks it again.

Can't I just power through distractions with more self-control?

Nir

I used to think so, but relying on sheer willpower is exhausting and unreliable. A better approach is to understand what drives the urge in the first place.

Nir

Once you notice what feelings spark distraction, like restlessness or anxiety, you can make intentional choices.

You

Isn't distraction mostly caused by technology?

Nir

Technology definitely makes it easier to get pulled away, but removing devices won't solve the problem.

If you delete social media, for example, that same urge will look for another outlet. Until you learn to deal with discomfort in a healthier way, distractions will always find you.

You

Why do small distractions matter if they only take a few minutes?

Nir

A quick glance at your phone, a short scroll through a feed, or a single email check may seem harmless, but each one breaks your focus.

Nir

Regaining this focus often takes much longer than the distraction itself. Over time, those little moments accumulate into hours lost.

Being Indistractable

At a glance:

★ **Distraction pulls us away from what we really want.**
Any action that pulls you off course from what you truly want is considered distraction.

★ **Traction moves us closer to our goals.**
Actions aligned with our intentions and values create progress and meaning.

★ **Triggers spark both traction and distraction.**
Triggers are cues that initiate behavior—some drive us forward, while others pull us away.

★ **External triggers come from our environment.**
Notifications, interruptions, and alerts are examples of cues that can lead to distraction if not managed.

★ **Internal triggers arise from within.**
Emotions such as boredom, stress, or anxiety often spark the urge to escape through distracting behaviors.

Being Indistractable

Each moment gives you a choice: to move toward traction or to drift into distraction. Traction is any action that moves you closer to your goals and values. Distraction is anything that pulls you away from them. The same behavior can fall into either category depending on whether it aligns with your plan.

Both traction and distraction start with triggers. External triggers come from your environment—notifications, buzzing phones, conversations, or ads—all trying to grab your attention. Internal triggers come from within, feelings like stress, boredom, loneliness, or fatigue. Distractions often start as an attempt to escape these feelings, while traction comes when your actions serve your goals.

Small choices matter. Answering email during the time you set aside for focused work may look productive, but it steals energy from the project that truly matters. The danger of distraction isn't only in obvious things like social media or TV—it can hide in tasks that look like progress but delay meaningful work.

To live with intention, you must notice the cues that lead you toward distraction and choose instead the actions that move you forward. This is what it means to be indistractable: keeping your commitments and making sure your time reflects your values.

To help you regain control of your attention, I created the four-part Indistractable Model:

1. Master Internal Triggers
Notice the feelings that spark distraction and learn healthier ways to handle them.

2. Make Time for Traction
Plan your day so your schedule reflects your values.

3. Hack Back External Triggers
Take control of the cues that compete for your attention.

4. Prevent Distraction with Pacts
Use precommitments to help you stick with your decisions.

The goal isn't to remove every interruption or silence every uncomfortable feeling. It's to build awareness, make deliberate choices, and create conditions that favor traction. Each time you choose traction, you strengthen your ability to live with intention and take another step toward being indistractable.

Exercise 2

Name one thing you did today that moved you
closer to what you really wanted, e.g., going to the
gym, focusing on an important task at work, etc.
Then list the benefit you received from that act of
traction, e.g., living healthfully, helping my team
close a sale, etc.

Exercise 3

We all know what it's like to have a distraction pull
us away from something that matters—whether it's
a moment with family, a critical point at work, or a
second to ourselves. When was the last time you
became aware of a distraction in your life? What did
the distraction take from you?

How to Be Indistractable

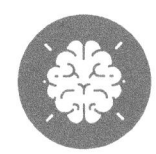

Master
Internal Triggers

Prevention
Distraction
with Pacts

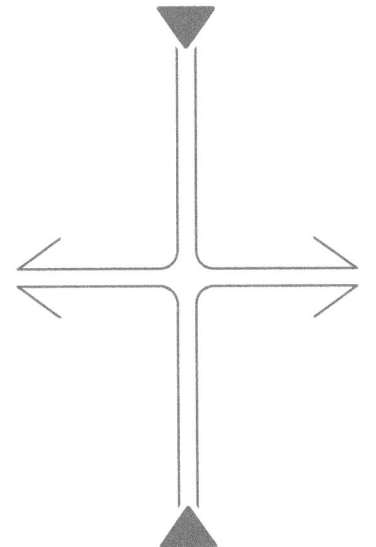

Make Time for
Traction

Hack Back
**External
Triggers**

Let's Chat! With Nir

You

> What does it mean to move toward traction instead of distraction?

Nir

> Think of traction as any action you do with intention that moves you toward your goals or values. Distraction is the opposite—anything that takes you further away.

Nir

> Watching a movie with family could be traction if that's what you planned, or distraction if it pulls you from something more important. The difference comes from whether the action serves what you intended.

You

> Why do you say that both traction and distraction come from triggers?

Nir

Every action starts with a cue. Sometimes it's an external one, like a buzz on your phone. Sometimes it's internal, like stress or boredom.

Nir

Both can lead you either toward traction or toward distraction. The important thing is noticing the trigger and asking if it's serving you or pulling you away.

You

Does that mean all notifications are bad?

Nir

Some reminders are really useful, like a calendar alert to depart for a meeting or a reminder to call a loved one. What matters is deciding which external triggers you want to keep to lead you toward traction.

Do I need to be perfect at this to call myself indistractable?

Absolutely not, and perfection isn't the goal. Distractions will still happen, but the difference is how you respond.

Being indistractable means noticing when you've been pulled away and returning to traction more quickly. Each time you do that, you strengthen your ability to live in line with your values.

Part

1

Master Internal Triggers

What Motivates Us, Really?

At a glance:

★ **Distraction is an escape from discomfort.**
We often assume technology is to blame, but the true source of distraction is our attempt to avoid unpleasant internal states.

★ **Motivation is driven by pain avoidance.**
All human behavior, whether constructive or destructive, is driven by the desire to relieve psychological or emotional discomfort.

★ **Temporary relief reinforces habits.**
When a behavior like checking messages or browsing online provides even brief relief, our brain learns to repeat it and strengthens the pattern.

★ **Potentially addictive does not mean irresistible.**
Any activity that reduces discomfort can become habit-forming, but this does not mean we are powerless to resist.

★ **Clarity creates control.**
By identifying the underlying discomfort that fuels distraction, you can intervene more effectively and adopt strategies that align with your long-term goals.

What Motivates Us, Really?

People often think their actions are driven by rewards or pleasure, but underneath those explanations lies a deeper truth: Most actions are driven by the desire to avoid pain. Whether it's physical, mental, or emotional, the desire to ease discomfort guides almost every decision we make.

For example, checking email can calm the worry of missing something important. Scrolling through social media can relieve boredom. Snacking can ease stress or fatigue. The action itself matters less than the comfort it brings. Once the brain associates relief with a behavior, the habit becomes stronger. Each repetition tightens the connection between discomfort and the action that reduces it.

This cycle can make us feel powerless in the face of phones, apps, or even coworkers. In reality, these are not the root causes of our distractions. So, when we remove one distraction, another quickly takes its place. That's why deleting apps or hiding devices rarely works for long. New outlets will always appear if the underlying feelings aren't addressed.

Even the pursuit of meaningful goals can follow the same pattern. Writing a book, training for a marathon, or chasing a promotion may also come from discomfort— feelings like restlessness, unease, or fear of regret.

In other words, both positive actions and distractions can be fueled by the same force: the wish to avoid pain.

Identifying this pattern is freeing because it makes distraction predictable instead of mysterious. The next time you feel the urge to break from your plan, ask: What discomfort am I trying to escape? By understanding behavior as a response to pain, you can redirect it with purpose and reclaim control over your attention.

Exercise 4

Refer back to the distraction you wrote down in the previous exercise. Write down three root causes of discomfort you may be trying to escape by succumbing to the unwanted behavior.

Example:

Distraction:
> Using my phone when I wanted to spend quality time with my daughter

Root Cause #1:
> Fear I might be missing out on something important at work

Root Cause #2:
> Anticipation of a client email

Root Cause #3:
> Boredom that accompanies playing with a young child for too long

Distraction:

Root Cause #1:

Root Cause #2:

Root Cause #3:

Let's Chat! With Nir

I've always believed people act because they want to pursue pleasure. Why do you say discomfort drives behavior?

Nir

Many people think we're motivated by rewards, but what actually drives us is the urge to ease discomfort. Hunger makes us eat. Boredom makes us pick up our phones. Anxiety makes us look for reassurance.

Nir

Fundamentally, it's the need to escape an uncomfortable feeling that drives action.

You

Does that mean all distractions come from pain?

Nir

Yes, in some form. It might be boredom, stress, loneliness, or uncertainty. Those feelings make us look for relief, and distraction offers it (at least temporarily).

Nir

Once we understand that connection, we can stop blaming the tools and start addressing the discomfort driving the urge.

You

If distraction eases discomfort, why should I fight it?

Nir

Quick fixes feel good now, but they jeopardize your progress. A notification that eases boredom for a moment leaves your real work unfinished.

True satisfaction comes from traction, which are actions that move you toward your goals, not from temporary relief.

How do I figure out what discomfort is driving my distractions?

Start by observing. When you feel the pull of distraction, pause and ask, "What am I feeling right now?"

Naming the emotion helps you see the real cause, and once you recognize the trigger, you can decide how to respond.

Time Management is Pain Management

At a glance:

★ **Time management is pain management.**
Distractions are often attempts to escape discomfort, not failures of scheduling alone.

★ **Relief is always temporary.**
Psychological tendencies such as boredom, negativity bias, rumination, and hedonic adaptation ensure that relief from discomfort never lasts.

★ **Dissatisfaction drives both progress and distraction.**
The same drive that makes us restless also fuels creativity, progress, and innovation.

★ **You can't escape discomfort.**
You cannot eliminate dissatisfaction, but you can choose healthier outlets rather than defaulting to distraction.

★ **Mastering discomfort protects our attention.**
Building resilience against internal discomfort is essential to protecting our time and pursuing meaningful work.

Time Management Is
Pain Management

Every distraction, big or small, usually starts with an uncomfortable feeling. We lose time not because we forget to plan or set reminders, but because we use distraction to ease discomfort. Fixing only the surface problem gives short-term relief, but it doesn't solve the real issue.

Think about when you grab your phone, open a new browser tab, or check your email. These may seem like random habits, but they all serve the same purpose: escaping restlessness, worry, or dissatisfaction. Distraction gives quick comfort, but it doesn't last. As soon as the comfort fades, the cycle starts again.

Feeling unsatisfied is part of being human. Our ancestors survived because their restlessness pushed them to keep searching, building, and improving. Today, that same drive can help us grow, but it also tempts us toward distractions that pull us off course.

Several mental habits make comfort short-lived and distraction tempting. Boredom makes stillness feel uncomfortable. Rumination keeps us replaying past mistakes or dwelling on future worries. Hedonic adaptation makes achievements feel less satisfying over time, leaving us constantly looking for the next high.

Distraction is less a failure of discipline and more a response to discomfort. That means managing your time comes down to managing your pain.

When you pay attention to the feelings that come before distraction, you learn to turn those internal triggers into cues for traction—actions that move you toward your goals. Discomfort will always be a fact of life, but with practice, you can consistently choose traction instead of slipping into distraction.

Exercise 5

Name three occurrences when you typically get distracted. For each occurrence, describe the distraction.

Example:

Occurrence:
Working on a big project

Distraction:
Checking email instead

Occurrence:

Distraction:

Occurrence:

Distraction:

Occurrence:

Distraction:

Let's Chat! With Nir

You

Why do you say time management is really pain management?

Nir

Because distraction usually isn't caused by a lack of planning tools. It's caused by the feelings we're trying to escape.

Nir

Stress, boredom, and dissatisfaction push us toward something that feels easier or more pleasant. Unless we deal with those feelings directly, no calendar hack or productivity tip will last.

You

Isn't feeling restless or dissatisfied a bad thing?

Nir

Not necessarily, because that same restlessness is part of what makes us inventive and ambitious. It drives us to explore, improve, and create.

Nir

The downside is that it also tempts us to escape into distractions. While we can't eliminate those feelings entirely, we can learn to guide them toward actions that serve our values.

You

Why doesn't relief from distraction last very long?

Nir

Our brains are wired to adapt quickly. That's why finishing one task or enjoying one reward often leaves us looking for the next.

Nir

Psychologists call this hedonic adaptation. The feeling fades, and the cycle of seeking relief begins again. Distraction can be satisfying in the moment, but it rarely sustains us.

You

What can I do when I notice myself seeking escape?

Nir

First, acknowledge what you're feeling instead of trying to suppress it. Naming the discomfort reduces its power.

Nir

Then, ask if the action you're about to take aligns with your values. If it does, it's traction. If it doesn't, consider how else you might respond to move you closer to your goals.

Deal with Distraction from Within

At a glance:

★ **Willpower alone isn't enough.**
Resisting urges through sheer self-control ("Just say no.") often backfires, intensifying the very desires you want to suppress.

★ **Avoidance fuels fixation.**
Avoidance strategies may increase fixation on the unwanted behavior, making distraction harder to resist.

★ **Reframing weakens temptation.**
By changing how you interpret internal triggers, you can reduce their pull and manage them more effectively.

★ **Change your relationship with discomfort.**
You can reimagine the trigger (how you perceive the feeling), the task (how you engage with the work), and the temperament (how you see yourself and your capacity for self-control).

★ **Curiosity beats control.**
Developing healthier perspectives toward discomfort allows you to respond with curiosity and compassion rather than avoidance.

Deal with Distraction from Within

Willpower alone is rarely enough to overcome distraction. When you try to push an urge away, your mind focuses more on it, and the craving grows stronger. The outcome is usually frustration and the sense that the behavior is in control, rather than you.

A more effective approach is to change how you respond to discomfort. Instead of struggling against urges, you can learn to notice them, examine them, and then choose how to act. Creating space between the feeling and your reaction allows you to consider a different path forward.

Distraction usually begins with internal triggers such as stress, boredom, or insecurity. Although these feelings are part of life, you have the ability to interpret and manage them in healthier ways. Recognizing that an urge is only temporary helps reduce its power.

When you notice these feelings and approach them with curiosity, you interrupt the automatic reactions that can lead to distraction.

Another way to handle internal triggers is to reimagine the task itself. When work feels dull or difficult, the mind searches for an escape. If you introduce a challenge or even a sense of play, the same task becomes more engaging.

The beliefs you hold about yourself also influence your behavior. Thoughts such as "I have no discipline" or "I'm addicted to my phone" create excuses to quit and reinforce negative labels. A more helpful approach is to speak to yourself with the same patience and care you would give a close friend. Self-compassion helps you recover from setbacks and makes you more resilient to future distractions.

Managing distraction from within involves paying attention to your urges, identifying the needs behind them, and responding with intention. Over time, these methods increase resilience and help you stay connected to your values.

Exercise 6

Recall one incident when mental abstinence—just saying no—backfired and left you further away from what you really wanted. For example: "When I went on an extreme diet, I gained back all the weight and then some."

Let's Chat! With Nir

Why isn't it effective if I tell myself to "just stop" when I feel distracted?

Because resisting an urge with brute force usually makes it stronger. The more you try not to think about something, the more your mind fixates on it. That's why simply relying on willpower often backfires.

If resisting doesn't work, what does?

The key is to change your relationship with the urge. Instead of fighting it, notice it. Observe how it feels in your body and mind.

That pause helps you realize the feeling is temporary and gives you room to choose how you respond.

What do you mean by reimagining the task?

When a task feels like punishment, your mind looks for escape. But when you reframe it with curiosity or play, the same task becomes more engaging.

Even something repetitive can feel lighter when you treat it as a challenge or an opportunity to learn.

How does self-talk influence distraction?

How you label yourself matters. If you tell yourself, "I have no discipline" or "I'm addicted to distractions," you reinforce those beliefs.

If you practice self-compassion and remind yourself that distraction is part of being human, you bounce back more quickly. Harsh self-criticism keeps you stuck; kindness helps you recover.

Reimagine the Internal Trigger

At a glance:

★ **Distraction starts with feelings.**
Every distraction is preceded by an internal feeling, such as boredom, stress, or anxiety, that sparks the urge to escape.

★ **Name the trigger to break the pattern.**
Writing down the emotion or discomfort that arises before distraction helps break automatic patterns.

★ **Observe discomfort without judgment.**
Exploring negative sensations with openness rather than self-criticism lowers their intensity and power.

★ **Liminal moments are danger zones.**
During transitional periods, like waiting in line, sitting at a red light, or switching between tasks, we are especially prone to distraction.

★ **Awareness creates choice.**
By recognizing and reimagining internal triggers, you can respond intentionally instead of defaulting to avoidance.

Reimagine the Internal Trigger

Every distraction begins with a feeling. Restlessness, stress, fatigue, boredom, or worry can spark the urge to escape. These internal triggers cannot be eliminated, but they can be reimagined. The way you interpret and respond to them determines whether they pull you toward distraction or allow you to return to traction.

The first step in handling these triggers is awareness. By slowing down and noticing the emotion that comes before the behavior, you disrupt the cycle of distraction. Naming the feeling and even writing it down—"anxious," "tired," "pressured"—makes it less overwhelming and easier to manage.

Once you identify the trigger, the next step is observation. Approach the sensation with curiosity rather than judgment. Pay attention to how it shows up in your body. Does your chest feel tight, your stomach unsettled, or your shoulders tense? When you explore the urge instead of resisting it, you prevent it from taking control of your actions. In many cases, the sensation fades when given attention rather than met with avoidance.

Distraction is particularly common during liminal moments, the transitions between activities. For example, waiting in line, sitting before a meeting begins, or pausing at a red light often triggers the habit of reaching for your phone. Recognizing these moments ahead of time allows you to plan healthier responses.

One particularly effective tactic of managing distracting moments is to delay the urge. When you feel the pull of a distraction, tell yourself you can give in after ten minutes. Often, the urge crests and fades before the time is up. This rule encourages patience with your impulses while giving you room to make a deliberate choice.

By reimagining feelings that lead to distraction, you build the strength to control them instead of being controlled by them. Each urge becomes a chance to practice curiosity and awareness. Over time, these behaviors strengthen your ability to act with intention and control your attention.

Exercise   7

Refer back to the distraction you wrote down in the earlier exercise, or think of another distraction you frequently experience.

What discomfort(s) or internal trigger(s) did you feel immediately prior to the distraction? (Check all that apply.)

☐ Afraid   ☐ Frustrated
☐ Worried   ☐ Angry
☐ Overwhelmed   ☐ Hungry
☐ Lonely   ☐ Embarrassed
☐ Jealous   ☐ Tired
☐ Bored   ☐ Excited
☐ Nervous   ☐ Insecure
☐ Sad   ☐ Anxious
☐ Guilty   ☐ Pressured
☐ Confused   ☐ Resentful

Other:

Exercise 8

What observations can you make about yourself when you feel the internal trigger(s) you checked off in the previous exercise? Be sure to avoid placing judgment on your actions—simply state your observations.

Example:

When I feel _____ *stressed* _____ ,

I tend to _____ *scroll news headlines* _____ .

When I feel _____ ,

I tend to _____

_____ .

When I feel _____ ,

I tend to _____

_____ .

Exercise 9

What liminal moments in your day tend to leave you distracted? For example: in between classes, in the bathroom, waiting for the elevator, etc.

1.

2.

3.

Let's Chat! With Nir

You

> How can I stop reacting automatically to these triggers?

Nir

> The first step is to notice them. Most distractions happen before we even realize it. By naming the feeling, like saying "I'm anxious" or "I'm restless," you weaken its hold. Awareness breaks the cycle.

You

> What do I do once I've named the feeling?

Nir

> Instead of rushing to escape it, approach it with curiosity. Pay attention to how it shows up in your body; the act of observing helps you realize the sensation will pass without needing distraction.

Why can liminal moments be a problem?

Liminal moments are the brief transitions in our day that can often trigger mindless checking of our phones or devices.

By noticing them, you can plan healthier responses, such as taking a breath, reflecting on your next step, or simply staying present.

What's a simple technique I can use when the urge feels too strong?

Tell yourself you can give in to the urge after ten minutes. Often, it fades before the time is up, and you can return to what matters.

Reimagine the Task

At a glance:

★ **Tasks can be reframed as play.**
   Even routine or monotonous activities can be
   reinterpreted in ways that make them more engaging.

★ **Play fuels focus.**
   Approaching work with a sense of play or challenge
   helps maintain attention and reduces the temptation
   to escape.

★ **Fun doesn't require pleasure.**
   A task reframed as play must simply capture interest;
   it does not need to be inherently enjoyable.

★ **Novelty keeps us engaged.**
   Adding small variations or challenges to tasks
   increases engagement and reduces the likelihood of
   distraction.

★ **Curiosity transforms your view of work.**
   Viewing tasks through a lens of curiosity and
   creativity transforms them from burdens to
   opportunities for traction.

Reimagine the Task

Tasks often feel unbearable because they seem boring or repetitive, not because they are truly difficult. When work is viewed as a burden, the mind naturally seeks an escape, and distraction becomes the easiest solution. The way out of this cycle is to reimagine the task itself.

Enjoyment is not limited to games or leisure: Any activity can spark interest when you approach it with curiosity. This does not involve bribing yourself with rewards in order to survive unpleasant work. Rather, it means looking at the task in a new way so that it can hold your attention long enough to finish it.

One effective approach is to treat work as play. Play is not always fun, but it is engaging. Athletes repeat drills for hours, musicians practice scales, and artists sketch forms again and again. What sustains them is not constant enjoyment but the ability to notice novelty inside repetition.

The same perspective can be applied to everyday tasks. Can you complete them faster than before? Can you adjust the process to make them smoother? Can you uncover a hidden skill within what you once thought was routine? When you frame work as an opportunity for discovery, dull labor turns into meaningful practice.

Deliberate focus strengthens this reframing, since bringing full attention often reveals novelty you'd otherwise miss. Concentration itself becomes rewarding, and interest builds as you stay with the work. Even repetitive activities can become meaningful when explored with deliberate focus.

Reimagining a task doesn't eliminate the effort required, but it does shift your relationship with the work. By approaching tasks with curiosity, you allow space for discovery and ease follow-through.

Exercise 10

Describe one frequent task you have to do that you see as boring, e.g., going to the gym, responding to emails, filling out paperwork, etc.

Exercise 11

What can you do to reimagine the task above to make it feel more like play? What small challenges, constraints, or novelty can you add to make it fun? Remember, play doesn't have to be enjoyable per se; it just has to hold your attention long enough to help you overcome distraction.

Let's Chat! With Nir

You

How do I make something dull feel more engaging?

Nir

Approach it with curiosity or treat it like play. Ask yourself: Can I find a new pattern here? Can I finish it a little faster than last time?

Nir

Even repetitive tasks can feel lighter when you see them as challenges or opportunities to explore.

You

Isn't play supposed to be fun? What if the work still feels hard?

Play doesn't always mean pleasure. It often means engagement. When a task holds your attention, even if it's challenging, it becomes satisfying and keeps your mind from wandering into distraction.

You

What if the task itself is something I truly dislike?

Sometimes the task won't change, but how you relate to it can. Reframing the purpose by seeing it as part of your growth, or as a step toward something important, can reduce the urge to escape.

The task may not become enjoyable, but it can become meaningful.

You

How does reimagining the task help with distraction?

Nir

When you find ways to deeply engage, your attention remains on the work instead of the urge to escape.

Nir

The more often you practice reframing tasks, the easier it becomes to stay with them and build traction.

Reimagine Your Temperament

At a glance:

★ **How you see yourself shapes what you do.**
The way you view your capacity influences how you respond to distraction.

★ **Willpower is not a finite resource.**
Believing that self-control can "run out" makes you more likely to give in to distraction.

★ **Negative labels promote distraction.**
Identifying yourself as having "poor self-control" or an "addictive personality" reinforces unproductive patterns.

★ **Self-compassion fosters resilience.**
Talking to yourself with the same kindness you'd offer a friend reduces stress and helps you recover from setbacks.

★ **Reframe your temperament to stay focused.**
By adopting a compassionate and capable self-view, you can enhance persistence and strengthen your ability to remain focused.

Reimagine Your Temperament

The way you see yourself has a powerful influence on how you behave. Many people believe willpower is limited, as though self-control drains away with use. Once willpower feels depleted, individuals allow themselves to stop trying or to give in to distraction. This belief is both inaccurate and damaging because it converts a temporary challenge into an excuse to abandon goals and commitments.

Research shows that willpower is not finite—it depends largely on your perception. Your ability to stay on task can increase or decrease based on how you frame the challenge and the strategies you use. When you understand self-control in this light, you stop fearing that it will vanish. Instead, you learn to manage it as you would any other feeling.

The stories you tell yourself also shape your behavior. Statements like "I lack discipline" or "I cannot resist distraction" reinforce a negative self-image, making those outcomes more likely. The brain tends to accept these labels and adjust behavior to match them. By contrast, when you view yourself as someone who follows through, you increase the chances that your actions will align with that belief.

Self-compassion is equally important. Everyone loses focus at times. The greater danger lies not in the distraction itself but in the shame that often follows. Harsh self-criticism makes recovery harder and fuels avoidance. Treating yourself with the same understanding you would give a friend helps you return to traction more quickly.

Reimagining your temperament means choosing a healthier narrative: You are not powerless, nor are you destined for distraction. Each time you notice yourself distracted and return to what matters, you build strength. Setbacks become opportunities to exhibit patience rather than evidence of failure.

Temperament is not permanent; it is shaped by your beliefs, your self-talk, and your willingness to keep practicing.

Exercise 12

Do you harbor any self-limiting beliefs about your abilities? For example: "I have a short attention span" or "I have an addictive personality."

Write down any labels you attach to yourself and consider whether they are actually serving you.

Exercise   13

If a good friend were struggling with a distraction
you often face, what would you tell them for
comfort or support?

Exercise   14

How does your response to moments of setback
or failure make you feel? Are you able to console
yourself with the same words you'd offer a friend?

Exercise 15

Self-compassion makes us more resilient by easing the stress that usually comes with setbacks. How can you change your future response to be more self-compassionate?

Let's Chat! With Nir

Why do I often feel like I don't have enough willpower?

Many people have learned to think of willpower as something that runs out, so the moment they feel drained, they assume they have no choice but to give up.

In reality, self-control rises and falls depending on mindset and context. When you see it as something you can influence, you stop treating low moments as failure and start managing them more effectively.

What role do labels play in distraction?

The stories you tell yourself become self-fulfilling. When you say things like "I have no discipline" or "I can't resist distraction," you strengthen those patterns. Your brain takes those labels as truth and shapes your behavior to match them.

When you choose an identity like "I keep my commitments" or "I follow through," your actions start to align with those values.

How can self-compassion help me stay focused?

When you strongly criticize yourself for getting distracted, it becomes harder to recover. Harsh self-talk adds shame, which often drives more distraction.

Treating yourself with the same kindness you'd offer a friend helps you reset and return to traction more quickly.

You

Why do I keep slipping back into distraction even when I know better?

Nir

Old patterns are powerful, and it takes practice to replace them. Each time you catch yourself and return to traction, you weaken the old habit and strengthen the new one.

Make Time for Traction

Turn Values Into Time

At a glance:

★ **Distraction is anything that displaces your plan.**
An action can only be identified as a distraction if it diverts attention from a planned or valued activity.

★ **No schedule means no clarity.**
Without a predetermined schedule, it becomes difficult to distinguish between traction and distraction.

★ **Your time should reflect your values.**
To live intentionally, we must allocate time to activities aligned with our core principles and priorities.

★ **Timeboxing promotes balance.**
Dividing the day into dedicated blocks for your well-being, relationships, and work ensures balance across life domains.

★ **Reflection keeps you aligned.**
Regularly reviewing and adjusting your schedule helps maintain consistency between values and daily actions.

Turn Values Into Time

You cannot call something a distraction unless you know what it is distracting you from. Traction requires a plan. Without one, anything can feel urgent, and every request from others can pull you in a different direction. To stay on track, your schedule must reflect your values.

Values are not abstract ideals. They are the principles that define who you want to be in each area of your life. They answer questions such as: What does it mean to care for yourself? How do you want to show up for your family and friends? How do you want to contribute at work? Values are not goals you achieve once; they are ongoing qualities you live out daily.

The problem is that many people leave their schedules blank. They may keep long to-do lists but never decide when those tasks will happen. A list without a calendar creates pressure, while timeboxing creates clarity. By giving every block of time a purpose in advance, you turn your values into time. When your day is guided by your values, you know at any moment whether you are on or off track.

There are three main domains in your life where understanding your values is pivotal: you, your relationships, and your work. You come first, because caring for your body and mind sustains everything else.

Sleep, exercise, meals, and personal growth deserve protected time on your calendar. Relationships come next. Family and friends cannot thrive on leftover time; they require deliberate attention. Work is the third domain, which includes professional duties, creative efforts, and service to others.

Once your week is mapped across these domains, review and refine it regularly. When did you follow your plan? When did you get pulled away? What adjustments will bring you closer to your values? Reflection turns scheduling into a practice of continuous improvement rather than a rigid set of rules.

A timeboxed calendar keeps you from drifting and creates boundaries that protect your time. When your schedule reflects your values, you live your day knowing that your time is spent on what matters most.

Exercise 16

Imagine your ideal daily routine. What would it look like, and how would you spend your time so that your actions truly align with your values?

Exercise 17

Compare your ideal daily routine to your current daily schedule. What could be improved? What should you make more time for?

Let's Chat! With Nir

You

Why do I need a schedule if I already know my priorities?

Nir

Because good intentions alone aren't enough. If your values aren't reflected on your calendar, the world will fill your time with other people's priorities. A schedule is how you ensure your time is spent on what matters most to you.

You

What's the difference between goals and values?

Nir

Goals are things you achieve, like finishing a project or running a marathon. Values are ongoing qualities that define who you want to be, like a caring parent or a healthy person.

Goals have an endpoint, whereas values guide you every day.

How does timeboxing help me live according to my values?

By assigning every block of time a purpose, you turn abstract values into concrete actions. If health is important, you set aside time to exercise. If family matters, you reserve time for them.

Without timeboxing, those things are often pushed aside by distractions or urgent tasks.

What if something unexpected comes up and my schedule changes?

Timeboxing isn't meant to be rigid. It's meant to keep you intentional. When circumstances change, update your calendar with the same thoughtfulness you used to create it.

The key is to stay deliberate rather than reactive. Even when plans shift, you can always come back to your schedule instead of letting distraction decide for you.

Control the Inputs, Not the Outcomes

At a glance:

★ **Focus on effort rather than results.**
Outcomes are often uncertain, but you can always
control the time and energy you invest.

★ **Prioritize personal well-being.**
Devoting time to self-care like sleep, exercise, and
reflection strengthens both your relationships and
your work.

★ **Consistency matters more than intensity.**
Showing up and honoring scheduled commitments
builds long-term progress.

★ **Make time for your values.**
Dedicating time to value-driven activities ensures that
effort contributes to meaningful growth, regardless of
the outcome.

★ **Attention follows intention.**
Designing your day around intentional choices
anchors your attention, even when external outcomes
remain unpredictable.

Control the Inputs,
Not the Outcomes

Many parts of life are outside your control. You cannot make yourself fall asleep the moment you want to. You cannot force a creative idea to appear. You cannot dictate others' perceptions of your project at work. However, while outcomes are often uncertain, you can always control the effort you give and the intention behind your actions.

Inputs are the steps you take and the actions you commit to. Outcomes are the results you hope will come from those actions. When you keep your attention on inputs, you reduce the stress of chasing results you cannot promise. You may not be able to control whether you drift off to sleep right away, but you can create the right setting for rest and give yourself enough time in bed. You may not decide when inspiration appears, but you can control showing up consistently and doing the work that makes creativity possible.

Focusing on inputs means keeping the commitments you place on your calendar. If you schedule time for exercise, you move your body; if you schedule time for writing, you sit down and put words on the page. Each time you do what you planned, you've succeeded: You did what you said you would do, regardless of the outcome.

When you measure success with inputs, you can take pride in following through and strengthen your resistance to distraction. By training yourself to see progress in your effort, you stop depending on immediate results for motivation. You learn to feel satisfaction from honoring your plan and create conditions for lasting success.

Exercise 18

Name the activities you want to do for yourself every week. Include all activities that serve your values, e.g., time for sleep, healthy meal preparation, personal development, etc.

Exercise 19

Now that you have your list, note how much time you'd like to allocate for each activity in a typical week.

Activity	Time I'd Like to Allocate Weekly
Example: going to the gym	7 hours (1 hour per day)

Let's Chat! With Nir

Why focus on inputs instead of outcomes?

Because you can't guarantee instant results, but you can control the effort you put in. When you measure success with inputs, like showing up or following your plan, you free yourself from chasing results you can't always dictate.

Doesn't this lower the bar for success?

By controlling the inputs, you link success to personal integrity. Did you do what you said you would? Over time, consistent inputs compound into better outcomes.

How does focusing on inputs build resilience?

It trains you to keep going even when progress is slow. When you take pride in showing up and honoring your plan, you don't need instant feedback to stay motivated.

That steadiness makes you less likely to quit when results take time.

What if I don't feel like following through?

This is when the calendar becomes your contract with yourself. You may not always feel motivated, but you can honor the time you reserved.

When you follow through on inputs, you strengthen your identity as someone who keeps promises, especially to yourself.

Schedule Important Relationships

At a glance:

★ **Relationships need scheduled time, not leftovers.**
Meaningful connections cannot thrive on leftover availability; they're built on scheduled time.

★ **Equity means making time for shared duties.**
Shared responsibilities, such as household tasks, should be included in the calendar.

★ **Friendships are vital for health and happiness.**
A lack of close social bonds can negatively affect both mental and physical health.

★ **Scheduling shows people they matter.**
Allocating regular time for family and friends signals their importance and helps prevent neglect.

★ **Consistency builds stronger bonds.**
Regular, reliable moments of connection build trust and keep relationships close.

Schedule Important Relationships

The people who matter most cannot thrive on scraps of time left after everything else is done. Strong bonds with family and friends require more than leftover attention. For relationships to grow, they must have a place in your calendar that is just as intentional as any meeting or personal routine.

Think carefully about your values in this area: Perhaps you strive to be a loving partner, an engaged parent, a dependable friend, or a supportive contributor at home. Without scheduling time for these values, even strong relationships begin to weaken.

Start with family and schedule consistent time with them. These occasions don't need to be elaborate—a weekly meal, a Friday game night, or a recurring date can provide the rhythm that relationships need. This way, time with family is protected and treated with the importance it deserves.

Friendships require equal care. Research shows that close connections are essential for our well-being, yet friendships often fade due to neglect.

Regular calls, gatherings, or shared activities help maintain connection. Planning these moments keeps relationships alive where spontaneity often fails.

Shared responsibilities also belong on the calendar. Household chores, kids' bedtime routines, and other daily logistics quickly become sources of conflict if left unplanned. Scheduling these responsibilities removes confusion and reduces resentment. When commitments are visible to both partners, balance and fairness are easier to achieve.

Your calendar reveals your priorities; if you value deep and lasting connections, they must be visible there. By consistently dedicating time to those you love, you strengthen those bonds, honor your commitments, and build a life where loved ones never feel secondary.

Exercise 20

Name the activities you want to do with, or for, the important people in your life each week. List activities that serve your values, e.g., time for playing with your kids, fun time with your significant other, conversations with friends, etc.

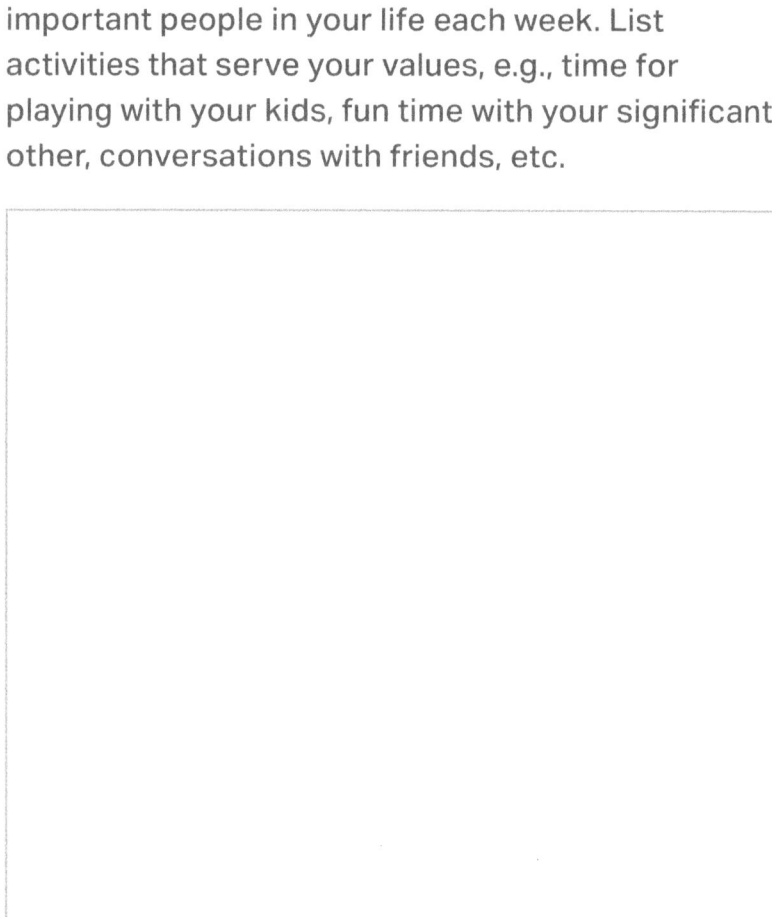

Review your list and make sure to include domestic responsibilities—tidying up, preparing meals, shopping for the family, etc.—as part of your commitment to your relationships.

Exercise 21

Now that you have your list, note how much time you'd like to allocate for each activity in a typical week.

Activity	Time I'd Like to Allocate Weekly
Example: time with close friends	2 hours every week

Let's Chat! With Nir

Why should I schedule time with loved ones instead of keeping it spontaneous?

Nir

Because if you don't protect that time, something else will take it. Work, distractions, and other people's requests always expand to fill the gaps.

Nir

Scheduling shows the people you care about that they matter as much as your other commitments.

You

Doesn't scheduling relationships make them feel less genuine?

Some of life's most meaningful experiences, like holidays, celebrations, and family traditions, are scheduled in advance. By putting loved ones on your calendar, you protect those moments from being crowded out by less important demands.

You

What kinds of activities should I schedule?

Nir

You can schedule anything that reflects your values. That might mean date nights, family dinners, bedtime routines with kids, or regular calls with friends.

Nir

It can also include shared responsibilities, like cooking or cleaning, so they don't become unspoken points of tension.

You

What if my schedule is unpredictable?

Nir

You can still block recurring time, even if you need to move it occasionally. The important thing is that time is set aside for fostering your relationships.

Nir

When you prioritize relationships on your calendar, you're more likely to protect them, even in a busy week.

Sync with Stakeholders at Work

At a glance:

★ **Visibility reduces unnecessary interruptions.**
When colleagues and managers understand how your time is allocated, they are less likely to impose unplanned tasks.

★ **Regular alignment keeps priorities clear.**
Frequent check-ins ensure that expectations remain clear and priorities remain consistent.

★ **Syncing schedules protects focus.**
Shared schedules enable focused work by minimizing miscommunications and surprise demands.

★ **Adjust how often you sync with stakeholders.**
The frequency of syncing should match how often your schedule changes—daily for fluid schedules or weekly for stable ones.

★ **Transparency fosters trust.**
Transparent scheduling creates mutual accountability and fosters a culture of respect for focused time.

Sync with Stakeholders at Work

Work takes up much of your waking life; if you do not guide how that time is spent, others will shape it for you. Managers, colleagues, and clients all have needs, and without clear expectations, their requests can quickly fill your schedule. Miscommunication creates frustration, and distractions multiply. The solution is to regularly sync with stakeholders so that priorities and boundaries are clear to everyone involved.

Stakeholders include anyone who depends on your work or whose expectations influence your day. If you fail to explain how you intend to spend your time, others may assume it is available for their needs. Over time, this creates a cycle of endless requests, unnecessary meetings, and a constant sense of urgency.

A timeboxed schedule is one of the most effective tools for alignment. Sharing your calendar makes your priorities visible. When your manager or colleagues see time reserved for focused work, meetings, and communication, their expectations become more realistic. Syncing ensures that you and your stakeholders agree on how time will be used, which lowers the risk of being pulled into low-value tasks.

Keep syncs simple: weekly for most roles, daily if priorities shift quickly. Use this time to review what you plan to accomplish, reflect on where distractions got in the way, and agree on any adjustments moving forward. These conversations build trust because they show that you are deliberate about your commitments and give stakeholders confidence in your progress.

Syncing also prevents misaligned priorities. Without it, you risk spending hours on work that others see as secondary, while urgent tasks remain unfinished. Regular alignment keeps effort connected to expectations, saving time and avoiding frustration.

Syncing with stakeholders offers the clarity and support needed to protect your time. By making alignment a habit, you create the conditions for deeper focus, stronger collaboration, and greater impact.

Exercise 22

Name the activities you want to do every week in the work domain of your life.

Review your list to make sure you've included reflexive work (answering messages, attending meetings, or answering calls) in addition to focused work (reviewing a long-term project, preparing a presentation, or proofreading a report).

Exercise 23

Now that you have your list, estimate how much time you'd like to allocate to each activity in a typical week. Make sure you reflect your personal values and the value you contribute to your company.

Activity	Time I'd Like to Allocate Weekly
Example: time for strategic thinking	2 hours every week

Exercise 24

Take some time to look at your schedule as a game or puzzle. The pieces of the puzzle are the time blocks you've now identified in each of your three life domains (You, Relationships, and Work).

Much like a game of Tetris, the mission is to arrange and rearrange the pieces of the puzzle in order to fit them into your schedule. Think creatively about how you can make things work. For example, what tasks can you eliminate or outsource? What tasks can you spend less time on? Can you batch similar tasks together?

Eliminate your preconceived notions of what an ordinary day should look like. After all, this is your game, your life, and, therefore, your rules.

(Use this free schedule maker tool to construct your day: NirAndFar.com/schedule-maker/)

Let's Chat! With Nir

You

Why do I need to sync with my boss or teammates if my calendar is already planned?

Nir

Your schedule doesn't exist in a vacuum. Others have expectations about your time, and if their expectations aren't aligned with yours, conflict and distractions follow. Syncing makes your priorities visible and creates mutual understanding.

You

What should I cover in a sync?

Nir

Share what you've planned, your top priorities, and any obstacles you're facing. Use this time to clarify which tasks truly matter to your manager or team so you can stay focused on traction.

How does syncing reduce distractions?

When your manager or colleagues see that you've set aside time for deep work, they're less likely to interrupt you with phone calls, meetings, or last-minute requests.

What if my manager keeps adding more than I can handle?

By reviewing your timeboxed schedule with your manager, you can have a productive conversation about trade-offs. If something new comes in, something else may need to be deprioritized. Syncs give you the structure to manage expectations without burning out.

Hack Back External Triggers

Ask the Critical Question

At a glance:

★ **External triggers often drive distraction.**
Notifications, alerts, and interruptions can easily pull attention away from intended work.

★ **Not all triggers are harmful.**
Some triggers can support traction by reminding you of commitments or guiding you toward valued actions.

★ **Check: Who's in control?**
Ask yourself, "Does this trigger serve me, or do I serve it?"

★ **Cut or control distracting triggers.**
When a trigger primarily leads to distraction, it should be removed, adjusted, or tightly managed.

★ **Keep and strengthen triggers that support traction.**
External cues that encourage focus or support long-term goals should be intentionally preserved or strengthened.

Ask the Critical Question

Every ping, buzz, and alert is designed to capture your attention. When a reminder nudges you toward an intended action—leaving for the gym, beginning a programming session, or joining a call—it creates traction. When a trigger interrupts your concentration or pulls you into something you did not plan, it becomes a distraction.

When presented with an external trigger, ask yourself the critical question: Does this trigger serve me, or do I serve it?

Simply trying to ignore unwanted triggers rarely works. Research shows that even the presence of a phone on your desk can drain mental energy, since part of your attention is devoted to resisting it.

Instead, hacking back external triggers means intentionally shaping your environment. Reduce triggers that lead to distraction and strengthen those that support traction. That might include disabling unnecessary notifications, putting your phone on Do Not Disturb, or keeping your devices out of sight.

However, not all external triggers are harmful; you can also design positive cues, such as reminders that guide you back to your priorities and reinforce your values.

Your environment is full of signals competing for your attention. Each time you hear a ding, see a banner, or feel the pull to check something, pause and ask the critical question. If the trigger helps you follow through, keep it. If it does not, adjust it or remove it. By deciding which external triggers to allow, you regain the ability to follow through on your intentions.

Exercise 25

Set a timer for 3 minutes.

Make a list of the external triggers you typically experience throughout the day. Think about what grabs your attention at home, at work, or with your family.

Next to each trigger, note whether:

- It served you (it helped you stay on track—traction)
- You served it (it pulled you off track—distraction)

External Trigger	Trigger Served Me	I Served the Trigger
Example: morning alarm clock	✔	
Example: phone call during work		✔

Let's Chat! With Nir

You

How does asking the critical question help me?

Nir

It gives you a simple filter. Each time a trigger shows up, you pause and ask whether it serves your goals. That quick check restores your power to choose.

You

What's the danger of leaving all my notifications on?

Nir

You're training yourself to be constantly reactive. Instead of following your schedule, you become a servant to every ping, ding, and ring.

You

Why isn't it enough to just ignore unwanted notifications?

Nir

Just seeing or hearing these notifications forces your brain to use energy in resisting. Over time, that constant resistance drains you. It's better to remove or reconfigure the trigger entirely.

You

How do I know which triggers to keep?

Nir

Keep the triggers that remind you of what you timeboxed in your day and support your values. Remove or mute the ones that push you toward someone else's priorities. When you choose your triggers with intention, you decide how your time is spent instead of letting others decide for you.

Hack Back Work Interruptions

At a glance:

★ **Interruptions lead to mistakes.**
Frequent disruptions increase mistakes and reduce the quality of work.

★ **Workplace design influences distraction.**
Open-office environments and norms of constant availability often amplify interruptions.

★ **Focus requires clear signals.**
Communicating when you are unavailable, through visual cues such as signs or indicators, helps protect concentration.

★ **Boundaries reduce intrusions.**
Setting explicit limits with colleagues or family members reduces unnecessary interruptions.

★ **Defend attention to do your best work.**
Proactively managing external triggers creates conditions for sustained, high-quality work.

Hack Back Work Interruptions

Interruptions are one of the most harmful forms of distraction. A single disruption can break concentration, increase mistakes, and waste valuable time. Even brief interruptions can derail us, making it harder to return to the task at hand. Protecting your ability to concentrate begins with building defenses against unnecessary intrusions.

Many interruptions come from colleagues who stop by with questions, requests, or the desire for casual conversation—scattering attention and blocking progress on tasks that require deep focus. Remote work brings similar challenges when family members or housemates do not recognize the impact of their interruptions.

The solution is not isolation but clear boundaries: Others must know when you are unavailable. A visible signal on your screen, desk, or door makes the boundary explicit. Though putting on headphones is a common choice, they're often overlooked; a clear sign is harder to miss.

For environments where interruptions are common, schedule specific times of availability. Let teammates know when questions, collaboration, or feedback are welcome. This approach reassures others that their needs will be addressed while protecting long stretches of uninterrupted work.

The design of your physical space also matters. Open offices make interruptions easier and increase the number of distractions. When possible, arrange your workspace to limit visual and auditory cues that pull your attention away. For those working from home, agreements with family or roommates about dedicated focus periods can prevent many disruptions before they begin.

The cost of interruptions is more than lost time—they raise the likelihood of errors and reduce the quality of your work. Hacking back work interruptions lowers mistakes, increases productivity, and gives you greater control over your attention in any environment.

Exercise 26

Think of the person who tends to interrupt you most frequently while you're working. Imagine the additional traction you could achieve each day in the absence of those interruptions.

Exercise 27

What cues will you use to let colleagues or family members know that you cannot be interrupted?

Suggestion: Make it clear when you're doing focused work by downloading your free *Indistractable* screen sign at NirAndFar.com/Indistractable/.

Let's Chat! With Nir

You

What are the most common sources of interruptions at work?

Nir

Often, it's colleagues who mean well and drop by with questions, requests, or small talk. In remote settings, it might be family members or roommates who don't realize how much they're breaking your concentration.

You

How can I signal that I need uninterrupted time without offending people?

Nir

Use a visible signal: a sign on your desk, a status indicator on your computer, or a Do Not Disturb block on your calendar. Clear signals remove guesswork and help others respect your time.

You

How can I stay available for collaboration without constant interruptions?

Nir

Set specific times when you're available for questions or collaboration. This reassures others that they'll get your attention, while also protecting your time for traction at work.

You

How does this help me become indistractable?

Nir

Each boundary you set communicates that your time matters. Eventually, colleagues learn to respect your signals, and you gain more consistent stretches of productive work.

Hack Back Email

At a glance:

★ **Unmanaged email erodes focus.**
Constantly checking and responding pulls attention away from meaningful work and creates hidden productivity costs.

★ **Clarify when replies are truly needed.**
Each message should be evaluated for when a reply is needed: immediately, later today, or within the week.

★ **Batch responses to protect focus.**
Scheduling specific times for responding to emails prevents constant interruptions and preserves focus.

★ **Cut down the number of incoming emails.**
Techniques such as setting office hours, delaying delivery, and unsubscribing from nonessential messages decrease unnecessary email traffic.

★ **Handle each message faster and smarter.**
Using tools and structured practices minimizes effort while ensuring timely replies.

Hack Back Email

Email is one of the most persistent sources of distraction in today's workplace. Messages arrive faster than you can handle them, each tempting you to check, respond, or otherwise click away from the work you intended to do. Without a clear system, email grows to fill the day and leaves little space for meaningful progress.

A simple equation explains the challenge:

Time spent on email = (Number of messages) x (Minutes spent per message)

Regaining control means addressing both parts of this equation. The first step is reducing the number of messages that reach you. One of the most effective ways to do this is by sending fewer emails yourself. Most emails spark a reply, which adds to the ongoing back-and-forth and keeps inboxes full. Before pressing "send," ask whether the email is truly necessary and whether it needs to be sent immediately. Another strategy is to unsubscribe from newsletters or promotional lists that no longer serve you, preventing a steady stream of future clutter.

The second step is reducing the time spent on each message. Constantly checking email fragments your attention and makes even simple communication more costly. A better approach is to batch responses into planned sessions. Begin with a quick scan in the morning to sort messages by urgency—those that need immediate action, those that should be handled today, and those that can wait for later in the week. When it's time to reply, you can move quickly because this sorting has already been done.

The guiding principle is intention: Email should serve your priorities rather than dictate them. By reducing the volume of incoming messages, batching your responses, and setting clear rules for yourself, you hack back email and reclaim time for traction.

Exercise 28

Open your inbox and pick three new emails. For each message, ask yourself, "When does this person really need a response?" Label each email by choosing one of the options below:

- Immediate: needs action right now (rare)
- Today: should be answered before the end of the day
- This Week: safe to reply within the next few days

Fill in the blanks with your last three emails:

Email from _____

☐ Immediate ☐ Today ☐ This Week

Email from _____

☐ Immediate ☐ Today ☐ This Week

Email from _____

☐ Immediate ☐ Today ☐ This Week

Exercise 29

Open your timeboxed schedule. Set aside time to handle urgent emails daily, and reserve a longer weekly block for less urgent messages. Resist the urge to respond to non-urgent emails immediately.

Exercise 30

Scan your inbox and look at the last few promotional emails or newsletters you received. For each email, ask, "Is this helping me live and work with intention?"

- If yes, keep it.
- If no, click Unsubscribe.

Each time you unsubscribe, cross off one icon below.

Let's Chat! With Nir

Why does email feel endless, no matter how much I check it?

Nir

Leaving your inbox open and checking it constantly is the biggest mistake. Every time you peek, your focus breaks, and it takes effort to get back on track.

You

Why does checking email feel so urgent even when it usually isn't?

Nir

Because an unread message feels like unfinished business. Your brain keeps thinking about it until it's resolved, which makes the inbox feel more urgent than it really is.

The best way to handle this is to plan specific times to check email so you're in control, instead of reacting the moment a new message appears.

You

What's the best way to stay on top of my inbox without letting it control me?

Nir

Batch your responses. Set aside specific times for email, then sort and tag messages by urgency: immediate, today, or this week. That way, you respond with intention instead of constantly reacting.

You

Won't people expect quick replies if I slow down?

By setting expectations through delayed delivery, clear boundaries, or office hours, you signal to others that you respond thoughtfully, not instantly. Most people will respect that once they understand your intentions.

Hack Back Group Chat

At a glance:

★ **Constant group chat kills focus.**
Endless real-time messaging often fragments
attention and prevents deep work.

★ **Pick the right tool for the message.**
Not every message requires an instant response;
selecting the right tool for the task reduces overload.

★ **Manage group chat notifications.**
Remove group chat external triggers by turning on
your Do Not Disturb feature within the app until you
are ready to participate.

★ **Set clear expectations around availability.**
Informing colleagues when you are and are not
accessible helps balance responsiveness with focus.

★ **Use group chat intentionally.**
Group chat enhances productivity when used for
specific, time-bound discussions rather than all-day
communication.

Hack Back Group Chat

Group chat can often feel like a meeting that never ends. Every ping and flashing message signals urgency, even if the content is unimportant. When chat runs in the background all day, it leaves little space for the sustained focus that meaningful work requires. To use these tools well, you must decide both when and how to engage.

A practical approach is to treat chat like a place you visit briefly rather than a channel you monitor constantly. Step in for specific conversations or updates, then step out so you can return to focused work.

Notifications must also be handled deliberately. Disable non-essential alerts and use Do Not Disturb features during focus blocks. Schedule times to review messages and let teammates know when to expect replies. This practice protects your attention while reassuring colleagues that their questions will be addressed.

Be selective—not every conversation requires your presence. If you are included in chats that rarely relate to your responsibilities, consider leaving them or muting notifications. Having fewer active channels means fewer distractions competing for your attention.

Complex or sensitive topics rarely belong in group chat. Without tone or context, misunderstandings grow; constant replies also interrupt deep thinking, making it harder to reach thoughtful decisions.

Encourage teammates to share detailed ideas in documents or reserve important conversations for meetings where participants can give their full attention. Chat works best for short exchanges and light coordination, not for deep problem-solving.

Used wisely, chat reduces unnecessary meetings and keeps teams connected. Used constantly, it fragments attention and creates stress. By hacking back group chat, you reduce misunderstandings, avoid unnecessary interruptions, and increase the quality of your decision-making.

Exercise 31

Recall the last notification you received from your group chat and answer the following questions:

What were you working on when you received the notification?

How did the notification make you feel?

Did the notification take you away from focused work?

How did you respond to the notification?

Did this external trigger serve you (move you toward traction), or did you serve it (move you toward distraction)?

Let's Chat! With Nir

You

Should I leave group chat altogether?

Nir

Not necessarily, because group chat can be useful for quick coordination or short updates. The key is to use it intentionally. Step in when you choose, then step out once your purpose is complete.

You

How can I prevent chat from consuming my day?

Nir

Set clear boundaries by deciding when you'll check messages and letting your team know. Staying logged in all day makes distraction inevitable.

You

What if I'm worried about missing something important?

Nir

Mute or leave channels that aren't directly relevant to your work. Keep notifications only for the groups where your input is truly needed, so you'll see what matters without being overwhelmed by chatter.

You

When is chat the wrong tool?

Nir

Group chat is the wrong tool for complex or sensitive discussions. Important decisions need focus and context, which chat rarely provides. Use it for lightweight exchanges, not for solving big problems.

Hack Back Meetings

At a glance:

★ **Unnecessary meetings drain attention.**
Without clear purpose and preparation, meetings often generate more distraction than value.

★ **No agenda, no meeting.**
Requiring a written agenda and briefing materials makes it harder to call unproductive or unfocused meetings.

★ **Meetings are for building consensus.**
Creative problem-solving is best handled individually or in small groups before a larger meeting occurs.

★ **Be fully present—don't multitask.**
Using devices during meetings to escape boredom undermines participation and reduces effectiveness.

★ **Limit device use to one shared tool.**
To encourage attendee engagement, limit device use to one central device for presenting or recording notes.

Hack Back Meetings

Few workplace habits waste more time than poorly managed meetings. Too often, they are scheduled without a clear purpose, lack structure, and leave participants disengaged. The result is familiar—misused hours that could have supported meaningful work. To hack back meetings, you need clear standards that protect attention and raise expectations for how time is used.

A meeting should be called to build agreement or to share information that cannot be delivered in any other way. Two requirements help ensure this: a written agenda and a proposed solution. Agendas define the problem to be addressed, while proposed solutions provide a starting point for discussion. Without both in place, the meeting should not proceed.

Brainstorming and early problem-solving work best individually or in small groups. This method prevents dominant voices from taking over and encourages a wider range of ideas. Larger meetings are most useful for aligning around decisions and clarifying next steps once options have already been explored.

Once a meeting begins, full attention is critical. Multitasking or checking email weakens both focus and collaboration. To minimize distraction, use only one shared device for presenting or taking notes—set aside all other devices.

Meetings should also respect clear time limits. As sessions stretch longer, attention fades and tangents increase. Short, well-structured meetings are often more productive than drawn-out ones. Protecting time in this way benefits everyone in attendance.

Not every meeting can be avoided, but you can shape how they run. With clear standards, meetings stop being default calendar entries and become intentional tools of coordination.

Exercise 32

Discuss the benefits of distraction-free meetings with your colleagues. What were their reactions?

Exercise 33

Propose the idea of a screen-free environment for your next team meeting. What was the impact of everyone's full attention on the effectiveness of the meeting? If asking colleagues feels uncomfortable, try leaving your devices at your desk and note the change in your focus and participation.

Let's Chat! With Nir

You

> Why do so many meetings feel like a waste of time?

Nir

> Meetings often feel unproductive because they lack structure. Too many are scheduled without a clear agenda or stated purpose, and people walk in unprepared.

Nir

> Without direction, the conversation drifts, attention scatters, and valuable work time slips away.

You

> Why is multitasking in meetings such a problem?

Multitasking signals disengagement and divides attention. Checking email or doing other work may feel efficient, but it undermines the quality of the conversation.

If everyone commits to being fully present, meetings become shorter and more effective.

How do I decline a meeting without damaging relationships?

You don't have to say no outright. Ask for the agenda and the proposed solution first.

If it's clear you aren't needed, politely suggest you'll skip but stay available for follow-up. This shows respect for their time and yours.

How do I encourage better meeting habits without sounding difficult?

Model the behavior: Ask for agendas before agreeing to attend, suggest time limits, and recommend smaller groups when appropriate.

These two requirements force clarity, raise expectations, and make sure the time spent together moves work forward.

Hack Back Your Smartphone

At a glance:

★ **Smartphones should serve you, not own you.**
The device is a tool, not a master, and must be
managed intentionally to prevent distraction.

★ **Remove unnecessary apps.**
Deleting applications that no longer provide value
reduces clutter and temptation.

★ **Move distracting habits to other devices.**
Shifting certain activities, such as checking social
media, to other devices helps limit compulsive phone
use.

★ **Redesign your home screen for focus.**
Moving or hiding "slot machine" apps reduces
mindless checking.

★ **Reclaim attention by controlling notifications.**
Adjusting alert settings and using features like Do Not
Disturb minimizes external triggers and preserves
focus.

Hack Back Your Smartphone

No device has more influence over your daily attention than your smartphone. It guides you, connects you, and provides instant access to information; yet this same tool can easily become a constant source of distraction if not managed carefully.

The first step is to remove what you no longer use. Many phones are filled with forgotten apps that serve little purpose yet still draw attention. Deleting them reduces clutter and minimizes unnecessary temptation.

The second step is to replace distracting apps with healthier alternatives. If social media or video platforms consume too much of your time, consider moving those activities to a laptop or computer. By separating them from your phone, you make their use intentional rather than habitual. Even small changes, like wearing a watch to check the time instead of unlocking your phone, prevent countless unnecessary glances.

The third step is to rearrange your home screen. Keep only the apps that reflect your values, such as connection, health, or learning; move attention-grabbing "slot machine" apps into folders or off the main screen. A home screen designed with purpose helps ensure your phone supports traction instead of distraction.

The fourth step is to reclaim control over notifications. Phones often come with notifications enabled by default, handing control of your attention to app makers instead of you. Take that authority back by turning off non-essential notifications and allowing only the most important apps to reach you. Use features such as Do Not Disturb or downtime settings to protect your attention during focused work and give yourself uninterrupted time to rest.

Your phone should be a tool that works for you, not a constant source of interruption. With a few simple changes, your phone can become a powerful device to help you stay focused, present, and in control of your time.

Exercise 34

Which statement feels most true right now?

☐ My phone mostly serves me.
☐ Sometimes I serve my phone.
☐ Too often, I feel like my phone is in control.

Do you need to schedule a Hack Back session?

☐ Yes
☐ Not yet

If yes, block 1 hour on your calendar.

Write down your scheduled session here:
Date: _ _ / _ _ / _ _   Time: _ _ : _ _

Select your intention for that session:

☐ Remove unused apps
☐ Replace distracting apps with desktop-only
   access
☐ Rearrange home screen
☐ Reclaim notifications (turn off non-essential
   alerts)

Let's Chat! With Nir

You

> Why do smartphones feel so tempting?

Nir

> The reason smartphones are so hard to resist is that they're deliberately designed to capture attention.

Nir

> Every app is built to compete for your time, and because your phone is often within reach, it's easy to get pulled in without noticing.

You

> Do I need to give up my smartphone to stay focused?

You don't have to throw away your phone or go on a digital detox to take control of your attention. The point isn't to abandon the device but to configure it so it serves your goals.

When you remove unused apps, move distracting ones off your home screen, and take back control of notifications, your phone becomes a tool for traction instead of a constant source of distraction.

How do I handle the apps that keep pulling me in?

Move them off your home screen or limit them to desktop use. Social media, games, or streaming apps are less likely to occupy your time if they're harder to access, and small bits of friction make a big difference.

What about notifications?

Most apps don't deserve the right to interrupt you. Turn off non-essential alerts and use features like Do Not Disturb to protect your focus.

That way, your phone stops buzzing for other people's priorities and supports yours instead.

Hack Back Your Desktop

At a glance:

★ **Digital clutter reduces focus.**
A messy desktop filled with files and icons creates unnecessary cognitive load.

★ **A clean workspace boosts clarity and efficiency.**
Storing documents in folders and maintaining a clean workspace reduces distraction.

★ **Turn off desktop notifications.**
System alerts, software updates, and chat requests should be disabled to protect attention.

★ **Your screen design shapes your mindset.**
A thoughtfully arranged desktop, including an intentional background image, can encourage focus and motivation.

★ **Capture your desktop transformation.**
Documenting a clean desktop helps reinforce the value of keeping your digital space distraction-free.

Hack Back Your Desktop

Your digital workspace is as important as your physical one—and just as easy to neglect. A cluttered desktop overflowing with icons, tabs, and alerts can easily pull you toward distraction. A clean desktop removes unnecessary triggers, helps you feel more in control, and makes it easier to stay focused on the task at hand.

The first step is to declutter your desktop. Move stray files into a single folder so they're accessible when needed but remain out of sight. Choosing a background image that invites focus rather than distraction adds another layer of support.

The next step is to manage notifications. System alerts, chat banners, and software pop-ups interrupt concentration whenever they appear. Turn off anything that doesn't serve your values and keep only the most essential alerts. Features like Do Not Disturb make it possible to protect long stretches of uninterrupted time.

The third step is to take control of your browser tabs. Every open tab is a subtle reminder of something unfinished, tugging at your attention and making it harder to focus. Instead of leaving them open, save information with bookmarks or a read-later app. Closing the extra tabs clears your screen and frees up your mind, allowing you to fully focus on the task in front of you.

A clear, intentional digital workspace lowers friction, reduces interruptions, and helps you stay engaged. When you hack back your desktop, you create conditions that consistently support depth, focus, and meaningful progress.

Exercise 35

Mark True or False:

☐ T   ☐ F   My desktop is organized in a way that helps me stay focused.

☐ T   ☐ F   My files and documents are tucked away so they don't distract me.

☐ T   ☐ F   I'm not interrupted by unwanted desktop notifications (updates, chats, etc.).

Take a screenshot of your current desktop and save it as your "Before" photo.

If you answered False to any statements above, timebox a session to:

- Declutter files and put them into folders
- Adjust system preferences to control notifications
- Choose a wallpaper that inspires focus

> Write down your scheduled session here:
> Date: _ _ / _ _ / _ _   Time: _ _ : _ _

Take a screenshot of your new indistractable desktop.

How does your new desktop make you feel?

Let's Chat! With Nir

You

> Why does a cluttered desktop make it harder to focus?

Nir

> Every file and icon is a visual reminder of something unfinished. Even if you're not working on it, your brain notices it.

Nir

> That creates mental noise and makes it harder to focus on the task in front of you.

You

> What's the simplest way to clear my screen?

Nir

The quickest fix is to sweep everything into a single folder and start fresh. Then, pull out only the files you truly need.

Nir

A clear background creates mental space and helps you focus without the constant tug of digital clutter.

You

Are notifications on my computer as distracting as on my phone?

Nir

Unnecessary notifications compete for your attention, whether on your computer or your phone. Even when you don't click them, part of your mind gets pulled away. Turning off non-essential alerts is one of the fastest ways to reclaim focus.

How do I deal with too many open tabs?

Instead of leaving tabs open, save articles and resources in a read-later tool or bookmark them. Closing tabs not only clears your screen but also frees mental space.

Hack Back Online Articles

At a glance:

★ **Avoid distraction traps.**
Endless articles and videos create opportunities for distraction and time loss.

★ **Tab overload undermines focus.**
Keeping multiple nonessential tabs open increases the likelihood of straying from the intended task.

★ **Save content for later.**
Protect your attention by separating content consumption from concentration.

★ **Bundle content with routines to stay motivated.**
Pairing saved content with routine tasks, such as exercising or commuting, makes consumption more purposeful.

★ **Curate what truly matters.**
Regularly review your saved content and remove items that no longer feel relevant.

Hack Back Online Articles

The internet provides limitless information with just a few clicks. Articles, headlines, and recommendations compete for your attention, each designed to pull you toward another link. What starts as a quick search often becomes hours of browsing, leaving you further from your original goal. To stay focused, you need boundaries for how you consume online content.

One effective method is to separate reading from working. When you find an article in the middle of another task, resist the urge to open it right away. Save it to a read-later tool instead. This keeps your attention on the work in front of you while still preserving the resource for later. It also prevents the clutter of open tabs, which scatter focus and leave part of your mind preoccupied with unfinished reading.

Another strategy is to bundle content with existing routines. Listening to saved articles while you exercise, commute, or do chores lets you consume the content without taking time away from your priorities. Pairing content with daily activities turns it into intentional learning instead of impulsive consumption.

Research can quickly devolve into procrastination without mindful curation. For example, my simple search for a reusable water bottle led to dozens of open tabs and ultimately no purchase decision. By setting clear limits on how long and when you will search, you stop yourself from falling into a spiral of endless browsing.

The internet will always offer more information than anyone can absorb. Saving articles for later, pairing them with routines, and setting limits on research transform article consumption into a tool for progress rather than a source of distraction.

Exercise 36

Open your browser and answer:

How many tabs are open right now? _____

How many of those tabs relate directly to the task you were working on today?

☐ All of them were essential
☐ Some were essential, some weren't
☐ Most weren't essential

Exercise 37

Try an app or tool to save articles or videos for later instead of leaving them open in tabs.

Did you install or set up a tool today?

☐ Yes
☐ Not yet

Exercise 38

Pair your saved content with other activities that usually feel like chores. This way, you reward yourself while getting things done.

List a few activities you could do while listening to or reading your saved content:

Let's Chat! With Nir

You

Can't I leave tabs open as a way to remind myself to come back to them later?

Nir

Multiple open tabs keep part of your attention tied up, even if you're not looking at them. Close them and trust your read-later system. A tidy browser clears both your screen and your mind.

You

How can I make time for online articles without getting distracted?

Nir

Bundle them with another routine, like listening to saved articles while making coffee or grocery shopping. Turning this into a planned habit transforms it from procrastination into traction.

You

How do I know when research has turned into procrastination?

Nir

Notice when you stop looking for answers and start wandering. Set limits, like a timer or a specific number of sources, so your search stays purposeful.

Nir

Once you hit your limit, return to your primary work.

You

How do I keep my saved articles from turning into digital clutter?

Saved content is only useful if you actually plan to engage with it.

Set a regular time to review your list and clear out anything that's no longer relevant. Curate what serves you, and delete what doesn't.

Hack Back Your Feeds

At a glance:

★ **Feeds are engineered for engagement.**
Social media and news feeds are designed to capture attention through endless scrolling and personalized triggers.

★ **Uncontrolled feeds drive distraction.**
Without active management, feeds continually pull you away from traction.

★ **Avoid the homepage.**
Skip the feed by bookmarking and visiting specific pages directly.

★ **Filter feeds to show only what matters.**
By filtering feeds to display only purposeful or value-aligned information, you reduce wasted attention.

★ **Choose when and how to engage with feeds.**
Controlling your access to feeds allows you to benefit from them without being overwhelmed.

Hack Back Your Feeds

Social media and news platforms are designed to keep you scrolling; what begins as a quick check can extend into hours. These feeds work because they tap into your psychology: They play on the fear of missing out, spark curiosity, and offer endless novelty. Unlike a book or a TV episode, feeds don't have natural stopping points. There is always one more post, one more headline, one more video—making feeds some of the most challenging external triggers to resist.

Many platforms open straight into feeds engineered to maximize engagement. To disrupt this endless cycle, create bookmarks that take you directly to the features you value, such as messages, groups, or specific pages.

Browser extensions and third-party tools can also remove feeds altogether or substitute them with something more aligned with your values, like a calendar or inspirational quote. This method removes temptation at the source and saves you from the constant effort of resisting.

Instead of opening social media whenever notifications appear, timebox your usage. You can then enjoy these platforms without guilt during your scheduled time to engage, knowing the rest of your day is protected.

Curation is another way to take back control. When you follow only the people and pages that reflect your values, you reduce noise and avoid getting dragged into clickbait, arguments, or distractions. A carefully curated feed helps you stay informed without being overwhelmed.

Feeds are not inherently harmful—they can provide connection, information, and entertainment when used deliberately. However, if not optimized, they often shape your attention more than you realize, pulling you into patterns of passive consumption. Hacking back feeds ensures you reclaim authority over how these platforms fit into your life and engage with intention.

Exercise 39

In the table below, list the platforms where feeds pull you in, e.g., Instagram, LinkedIn, YouTube, etc.

For each platform, check off at least one way to hack back your feed:

- Remove It: Use a tool to block or replace distracting feeds
- Bypass It: Bookmark only the pages you need
- Limit It: Timebox when you'll allow yourself to scroll intentionally

Feed	Remove It	Bypass It	Limit It
Example: Instagram			✔

Exercise 40

Recall the three sources of all distraction:

- Internal Triggers: Did you feel boredom, stress, loneliness, fatigue, or frustration?
- External Triggers: Was it a ping, ding, phone call, colleague, or something in your environment?
- Planning Problems: Were you unclear about what you were supposed to be doing?

To discover what's taking you off track, log each time you find yourself distracted today on the following pages. Then, review your moments of distraction and add solutions to prevent them tomorrow.

Time: | 2 : | 5
Distraction: _____ Checked the news _____
Your Feelings: _____ Anxious, Bored _____
Distraction Type:
☒ Internal ☐ External ☐ Planning Problem
Future Solutions: ____ Surf the urge _____
_____

Time: _ _ : _ _
Distraction: _____
Your Feelings: _____
Distraction Type:
☐ Internal ☐ External ☐ Planning Problem
Future Solutions:_____
_____
_____

Time: _ _ : _ _
Distraction: _____
Your Feelings: _____
Distraction Type:
☐ Internal ☐ External ☐ Planning Problem
Future Solutions:_____
_____
_____

Time: _ _ : _ _
Distraction: _____
Your Feelings: _____
Distraction Type:
☐ Internal ☐ External ☐ Planning Problem
Future Solutions:_____
_____
_____

Time: _ _ : _ _
Distraction: _____
Your Feelings: _____
Distraction Type:
☐ Internal ☐ External ☐ Planning Problem
Future Solutions: _____
_____
_____

Time: _ _ : _ _
Distraction: _____
Your Feelings: _____
Distraction Type:
☐ Internal ☐ External ☐ Planning Problem
Future Solutions: _____
_____
_____

Time: _ _ : _ _
Distraction: _____
Your Feelings: _____
Distraction Type:
☐ Internal ☐ External ☐ Planning Problem
Future Solutions: _____
_____
_____

Time: _ _ : _ _
Distraction: _____
Your Feelings: _____
Distraction Type:
☐ Internal ☐ External ☐ Planning Problem
Future Solutions:_____
_____
_____

Time: _ _ : _ _
Distraction: _____
Your Feelings: _____
Distraction Type:
☐ Internal ☐ External ☐ Planning Problem
Future Solutions:_____
_____
_____

Time: _ _ : _ _
Distraction: _____
Your Feelings: _____
Distraction Type:
☐ Internal ☐ External ☐ Planning Problem
Future Solutions:_____
_____
_____

Let's Chat! With Nir

Why are feeds so hard to pull away from?

Feeds are engineered for endless engagement. Every scroll brings something new, which keeps your brain hooked on the promise of the next surprise. That design makes it easy to lose track of time.

Should I stop using social media and news feeds completely?

These platforms can keep you informed, entertained, and connected to others. The problem isn't that they exist, but how you use them.

If you let algorithms decide for you, you'll end up spending more time scrolling than you intended. But when you set limits and choose when to engage, feeds can serve your values instead of distracting you from them.

You

Why don't I feel satisfied after scrolling through my feed?

Nir

Feeds are designed to keep you hooked. Each swipe delivers a little novelty but never real closure.

Nir

Without natural stopping points, your brain keeps looking for the next thing, leaving you feeling unsatisfied. The key is to set your own limits so you decide when you're done, not the feed.

What's the role of timeboxing here?

Timeboxing turns scrolling from a mindless habit into an intentional activity. By scheduling when and how long you'll check feeds, you get the benefit of connection and updates without letting it spill over.

Prevent Distraction with Pacts

The Power of Precommitments

At a glance:

★ **Precommitments solidify your intentions.**
By making decisions in advance, you reduce the likelihood of succumbing to distraction in the moment.

★ **Start with the foundations.**
Precommitments are most effective after mastering internal triggers, managing external triggers, and timeboxing for traction.

★ **Limiting future choices reduces temptation.**
Structuring environments and creating commitments in advance reduces the temptation to engage in unwanted behaviors.

★ **Pacts strengthen commitment.**
Apply pacts toward personal growth, relationships, and professional responsibilities.

★ **Being indistractable requires self-regulation.**
Beyond removing distractions, you must proactively constrain your future behavior.

The Power of Precommitments

Even with clear intentions, temptation can feel overwhelming in the moment. You may plan to stay focused, but when discomfort or distraction appears, the urge to give in can be difficult to resist. Precommitments address this challenge by solidifying decisions ahead of time, reducing the chance of impulsive behavior later.

You've probably already used precommitments without realizing it. Maybe you deleted a food delivery app from your phone because you wanted to eat healthier, or put down a deposit for an online course you've been wanting to take. These small acts serve as financial, social, or logistical nudges; when temptation arises or an internal impulse kicks in, you've already made the choice that aligns with your values.

While precommitments can be powerful tools, they are not the first step: Before using them, you must learn to manage internal triggers, make time for traction, and hack back external triggers. Once those foundations are in place, precommitments add an extra layer of defense.

These commitments take many forms, such as creating friction that makes distractions harder to reach or attaching financial or social costs to giving in. Each method increases the distance between intention and impulse.

However, precommitments should be applied carefully. If they are too rigid, they may cause frustration or even backfire when they become impossible to maintain. When used thoughtfully, they remove distracting options ahead of time, making life easier for your future self.

Exercise 41

Recall a precommitment you made that successfully moved you toward traction in the "You" domain, e.g., enrolling in college or signing up for sessions with a personal trainer. Why do you think this precommitment worked for you?

Exercise 42

Recall a precommitment you made that successfully moved you toward traction in the "Relationship" domain, e.g., booking a babysitter for date night or planning a weekend getaway in advance. Why do you think this worked for you?

Exercise 43

Recall a precommitment you made that successfully moved you toward traction in the "Work" domain, e.g., announcing a product launch date or volunteering to run a training session. Why do you think this worked for you?

Let's Chat! With Nir

What exactly is a precommitment?

A precommitment is a decision made in advance to stick to your intentions by limiting your future choices. Instead of relying on self-control in the moment, you use forethought to stay on track.

Whether it's turning on Do Not Disturb before bed, blocking certain apps during work hours, or planning your day with timeboxed tasks, precommitments lower the chances that you'll give in to temptation.

Why are precommitments so effective?

Precommitments create space between your present intentions and future impulses, using forethought as a buffer.

When distraction shows up later, the choice has already been made. You've protected your future self from having to negotiate with temptation in the moment.

Aren't precommitments restrictive?

It may feel that way at first, but they actually create freedom by reducing your mental load. By removing unhelpful options, you protect your time and attention for what matters most.

When should I use a precommitment?

Precommitments work best when temptation is predictable and patterns of distraction are familiar. Use them in situations where you think you're likely to slip: staying up scrolling, skipping the gym, or checking email instead of working on a big project.

They're not the first line of defense, but a reinforcement strategy. Precommitments are a way to protect your intentions when you're most vulnerable to going off track.

Prevent Distraction
with Effort Pacts

At a glance:

★ **Effort pacts raise the barrier to distraction.**
By making unwanted behaviors more difficult, you
reduce the likelihood of giving in to them.

★ **Accountability partners keep you focused.**
Working alongside a peer or colleague creates visible
pressure to remain on task.

★ **Technology can support self-control.**
Tools can be used to help restrict access to
distracting apps or websites.

★ **Visibility strengthens discipline.**
Knowing that others can observe your behavior
or that systems are in place to block distractions
reduces the appeal of avoidance.

★ **Create a structured safeguard.**
By adding friction to undesired activities, you support
an environment that favors traction over distraction.

Prevent Distraction
with Effort Pacts

An effort pact is a form of precommitment: an agreement you make in advance to raise the stakes and make unwanted behaviors harder to access. This approach works because many distractions thrive on ease and immediacy. By making these behaviors less convenient, you reduce the likelihood of acting on impulse.

Effort pacts function by adding friction between you and the behavior you want to avoid. If you want to stop checking your phone at night, leave it in another room to charge. If you want to cut back on binge-watching, log out of your streaming account after each use. These small barriers force a pause, giving you time to reconsider before acting.

Technology can support these commitments; website blockers, app timers, and focus tools add resistance to digital distractions. Disrupting the automatic reflex of opening apps or visiting familiar sites creates space for you to decide whether the action aligns with your values.

Working alongside someone else is another powerful form of a precommitment. Whether in person or virtually, having an accountability partner raises the cost of straying from your intentions. Knowing that another person can see your behavior and expects you to uphold your commitment makes it harder to justify distraction.

These pacts are especially helpful when internal triggers feel strongest. Discomfort often drives the urge for quick relief, but added friction slows you down just enough to notice the impulse—creating the opportunity to choose traction.

Exercise 44

Recall the last time you found yourself distracted. What unintended behavior did you perform instead of staying on track?

Exercise 45

Using the above as an example, how might you leverage an effort pact to fend off distraction?

Exercise 46

Write down one long-term project or goal you're working on:

```
┌─────────────────────────────────────┐
│                                     │
│                                     │
│                                     │
│                                     │
│                                     │
└─────────────────────────────────────┘
```

Name one person who could help hold you accountable:

```
┌─────────────────────────────────────┐
│                                     │
└─────────────────────────────────────┘
```

How will this person help you stay on track? (Select one or add your own.)

```
┌─────────────────────────────────────┐
│  ☐  Check in with me regularly      │
│  ☐  Co-work with me (in person or virtually) │
│  ☐  Remind me of my commitment when I get │
│     distracted                      │
│  ☐  Other: _____ │
└─────────────────────────────────────┘
```

Reach out to your accountability partner to finalize the pact.

```
┌─────────────────────────────────────┐
│  Date: _ _ / _ _ / _ _              │
│  Your Signature: _____  │
│  Partner's Signature: _____  │
└─────────────────────────────────────┘
```

Let's Chat! With Nir

How do I know if an effort pact is right for me?

Effort pacts are most useful when you've already mastered the basics: managing internal triggers, making time for traction, and hacking back external triggers.

If you notice certain distractions keep slipping through despite those steps, an effort pact can serve as your safeguard.

Do effort pacts only work for digital distractions?

While tools like website blockers and app timers are common examples, effort pacts can also apply offline.

Leaving your phone in another room, storing tempting snacks out of sight, or arranging to meet a friend for a workout are all non-digital effort pacts.

How do effort pacts connect to identity?

Each time you use an effort pact to resist distraction, you reinforce the identity of someone who follows through. Over time, these small wins strengthen not just your focus but also your belief that you are indistractable.

What role do other people play in effort pacts?

Having an accountability partner adds social effort. You're less likely to break your focus when someone else can see what you're doing, and the extra layer of visibility strengthens your commitment.

Prevent Distraction
with Price Pacts

At a glance:

★ **Price pacts reinforce intentionality.**
   Price pacts heighten forethought by encouraging you
   to align your intentions with your actions.

★ **Financial stakes solidify commitments.**
   When money is at risk, you place greater importance
   on your commitment and increase your likelihood of
   following through.

★ **Know when to use price pacts.**
   Price pacts work most effectively when addressing
   temporary or clearly defined behaviors.

★ **Cut triggers to improve success rates.**
   Eliminating cues that lead to distraction increases the
   likelihood that the financial pact will succeed.

★ **Pair price pacts with self-compassion.**
   Before adopting a strategy that carries penalties,
   learn to treat yourself with kindness when facing
   setbacks.

Prevent Distraction
with Price Pacts

A price pact introduces a financial consequence for distraction. By placing money at risk, you increase the stakes of staying focused and choose traction over distraction.

This method works because people are especially sensitive to loss. Studies show that the pain of losing money is stronger than the pleasure of gaining the same amount. A price pact leverages this tendency by attaching a cost to distraction that you would rather avoid.

These pacts work best for short-term, specific goals. For instance, you might commit to tearing up a $50 bill if you check social media before finishing your paper. The consequence is clear and immediate, leaving little room for rationalization or excuse.

Immediacy is the key advantage of this approach. Long-term rewards such as career success or better health may feel distant in the moment, but the threat of losing money today feels urgent. That urgency helps sustain focus when temptation is strong.

However, pairing price pacts with self-compassion is essential. A single lapse does not mean total failure—the financial loss is a signal to adjust, not proof that you are incapable. Over time, the discomfort of paying the price reinforces your motivation to stay aligned with your goals.

By attaching a tangible cost to distraction, your goals shift from vague intentions to concrete commitments. Used wisely, price pacts serve as a powerful incentive to maintain focus in moments of temptation.

Exercise 47

What is one action or habit you want to follow through on, but often get distracted from?

Based on what you learned, do you think a price pact could be useful for this behavior?

- ☐ Yes. The behavior is time-bound, and I can control the triggers.
- ☐ No. The behavior is ongoing or influenced by things outside my control.
- ☐ Maybe. I'm unsure, but I'd like to try.

How much money (or what valuable resource) would motivate you to stay on track?

$ _____

Other resource:_____

Who will hold the money (or enforce the pact)?

_____

How do you feel about making a price pact for this goal?

What do you hope to gain by following through with this price pact?

Let's Chat! With Nir

You

> What kinds of behaviors are best suited for price pacts?

Nir

> They work best for short-term or clearly defined actions. For example, you might commit to losing money if you skip your weekly meal prep, stay up later than you planned watching TV, or scroll social media during work hours.

Nir

> Because the boundaries are specific and easy to measure, the cost feels immediate, and the pact is harder to rationalize away.

You

> Do I always need to risk money?

The principle behind a price pact is to attach a meaningful cost to distraction that feels just irritating enough to keep you on track without being so harsh that you give up altogether.

That cost doesn't have to be money. It could be your time, a privilege you value, or even agreeing to do something mildly uncomfortable if you don't follow through.

How much money should I put on the line?

The amount doesn't need to be huge, but it needs to sting. If the sum feels too small, you'll ignore it. If it feels too large, you'll avoid making the pact in the first place.

What if I break the pact? Does that mean I failed?

Slipping once doesn't make you a failure. The cost you pay is a reminder, not a judgment.

What matters is learning from it and deciding how to adjust your approach next time.
Over time, the price pact strengthens your commitment to stay indistractable.

Prevent Distraction with Identity Pacts

At a glance:

★ **Identity shapes our behavior.**
We tend to act in a way that is consistent with how we perceive ourselves.

★ **Identity pacts align actions with values.**
Adopting a chosen identity sets the standard you hold yourself to.

★ **Language signals ownership.**
Using phrases like "I don't" instead of "I can't" reinforces that the behavior is a choice, not a restriction.

★ **Sharing your identity builds accountability.**
Telling others about your commitment further reinforces the behavior and normalizes it socially.

★ **Rituals reinforce who you choose to be.**
Practices such as repeating affirmations, maintaining a timeboxed schedule, or adopting routines reinforce your chosen identity.

Prevent Distraction
with Identity Pacts

The strongest precommitments are those tied to identity. An identity pact works by helping your actions match the type of person you believe you are.

For example, someone who sees themselves as an athlete is more likely to stick to a workout routine. Someone who sees themselves as an environmentalist tends to make eco-friendly choices. Similarly, if you see yourself as the kind of person who follows through and maintains focus, staying on task feels like being true to your identity.

Language plays an important role in this process. Saying "I don't..." instead of "I can't..." shows ownership; for example, "I don't check social media during work hours" frames the decision as part of your identity. By contrast, "I can't check social media during work hours" suggests restriction and creates resistance. These small differences in wording signal whether the choice belongs to you or feels forced upon you.

Sharing your chosen identity makes it even stronger. When you tell colleagues, friends, or family about your identity, you create social accountability and feel motivated to live up to the image you present.

Rituals and reminders also support identity pacts. A morning affirmation, a note on your desk, or a daily review of your timeboxed schedule can reinforce the self-image you want to embody. These practices keep your chosen identity present in your mind and guide you back to traction when temptation appears.

Identity pacts differ from effort and price pacts because they do not depend on extra friction or financial penalties. Instead, they draw strength from belief. When you remind yourself of your new identity, such as "I am indistractable," you give your future self a clear standard to live by.

Your actions are shaped by the story you tell yourself. By choosing an identity aligned with your values, you direct your behavior toward what matters most. Each decision that reflects your chosen identity strengthens both your present self and the person you want to become.

Exercise 48

Fill in the blank below with your chosen identity.

Example:

"I am ___someone who keeps their word___."
"I am ___indistractable___."

"I am _____."

Exercise 49

When facing temptation, practice swapping "I can't" with "I don't."

Example:

Instead of: "I can't ___check social media at work___."
Say: "I don't ___check social media at work___."

Instead of: "I can't_____."
Say: "I don't_____."

Instead of: "I can't_____."
Say: "I don't_____."

Exercise 50

List one person, such as a friend, partner, or colleague, with whom you can share your new identity pact.

Exercise 51

Choose the rituals you'll use to strengthen your new identity. (Check all that apply.)

☐ Morning mantra or affirmation
☐ Timeboxed calendar review
☐ Visual reminder (sticky note, T-shirt, phone background, etc.)
☐ Other: _____

Exercise 52

How does declaring this identity make you feel?

Let's Chat! With Nir

How does identity shape my behavior?

Your brain works hard to stay consistent with the story you tell yourself. If you say, "I have no self-control," your actions will reinforce that story.

By contrast, if you say, "I'm someone who follows through," you're more likely to act in line with that belief.

What if I don't fully believe my new identity yet?

Each time you act in line with your chosen identity, you strengthen it. Over time, small, consistent actions add up until the identity feels natural instead of forced.

Can I have more than one identity pact?

Yes, this is quite common! You may choose to see yourself as indistractable at work, a reliable partner at home, and a consistent athlete in your fitness routine.

The key is to choose identities that align with your values and help guide your behavior; each identity pact reminds you of the person you want to be.

You

What makes identity pacts different from other precommitments?

Nir

Effort and price pacts rely on added friction or financial stakes. Identity pacts rely on belief. They're internalized, not imposed.

Nir

When you adopt an identity like being indistractable, you change how you see yourself. You become someone who follows through, takes control of their attention, and builds the life they want to live.

What Comes Next

Congratulations!

You've uncovered your distraction patterns, learned how to respond instead of react, and put systems in place to protect your time and values.

I am honored that you have completed this workbook and grateful for the honesty, effort, and commitment you brought to the process.

Distraction won't disappear forever—life will still bring interruptions and competing demands. However, next time distraction inevitably appears, you'll be equipped with a framework for reflection and recalibration.

Stay indistractable,

Nir

For more *Indistractable* tools and resources, visit:

NirAndFar.com/Indistractable/